P9-CDH-254

THE GARDENER'S QUOTATION BOOK

The Gardener's Quotation Book

A Literary Harvest

Edited by
JENNIFER TAYLOR

BARNES & NOBLE BOOKS
NEW YORK

This edition published by Marboro Books Corp.,
a division of Barnes & Noble, Inc.,
by arrangement with Robert Hale, Ltd.

1992 Barnes & Noble Books

ISBN 0-88029-882-0

Printed and bound in the United States of America

M 9 8 7 6 5 4 3 2 1

Preface

S every gardener knows, gardening is hard, backbreaking and at times disheartening work. One could call it outdoor housework such is the number of routine tasks that need to be done. The beauty of a well-hoed bed and freshly turned over soil lasts just until the birds and the cats come. There is the gauntlet of pests and diseases to run, and the vagaries of the weather to contend with.

But as every gardener also knows, gardening is relaxing, creative and satisfying. It seems to fulfil a human need to remain in touch with nature. For many centuries the word 'Paradise', which comes from the Persian, was used to mean a beautiful garden.

As a leisure activity gardening is ever growing in popularity, and the division of labour between men and women is thought to be fairly even. Although at various times in history care for the garden was considered the woman's responsibility, in Victorian times books had to be written to encourage ladies to take exercise with some gentle hoeing, and even digging – which is still often considered 'man's work', together with mowing the lawn. Gardening in a long, billowing skirt cannot have been easy.

There have been numerous fashions in gardening style, and

the debate between classical and romantic schools of gardening has at times been fierce. Perhaps the best gardens are a balance, combining formality of structural design with informality in planting.

When you are sitting by the fire on cold, wet and dark evenings, and get tired of reading about the glories promised in seedsmen's catalogues, you can dip into advice and observations from some of the great gardeners from John Evelyn *to* Gertrude Jekyll*; wallow in descriptions of summer gardens by Dickens,* George Eliot *and* D.H. *Lawrence; read of the experiences of* Gilbert *White, Rider Haggard and others who kept garden diaries. Can any gardener have suffered as many mishaps as* Fanny *Burney's husband* M. *d'*Arblay*? And you will find invaluable advice on different types of manure among other early garden lore.*

In Ruth Draper's famous sketch, a hostess showing guests round her garden apologizes for the fact that there is nothing in bloom. 'You should have seen it last week' is a popular refrain amongst gardeners, who are by nature an optimistic breed – next week, next month, next year will always be better. It will, if gardeners tend their gardens well, and I am tempted to add to Voltaire's *famous injunction in* Candide *by saying that the world would be a far better place if everyone mulched their gardens with old mushroom bed compost.*

JENNIFER TAYLOR

God Almightie first planted a Garden. And indeed, it is the Purest of Humane pleasure. It is the Greatest Refreshment to the Spirits of Man.

FRANCIS BACON
Essays

The kiss of the sun for pardon,
The song of the birds for mirth,
One is nearer God's heart in a garden
Than anywhere else on earth.

DOROTHY FRANCES GURNEY
'Garden Thoughts'

And the Lord God planted a garden eastward in Eden ... And out of the ground made the Lord God to grow every tree that is pleasant to the sight, and good for food ... And a river went out of Eden to water the garden ...

GENESIS 2:8–10

The very act of planting a seed in the earth has in it to me something beautiful ... I watch my garden beds after they are sown, and think how one of God's exquisite miracles is going on beneath the dark earth out of sight.

CELIA THAXTER
My Island Garden

I think that if ever a mortal heard the voice of God it would be in a garden at the cool of the day.

F. FRANKFORT MOORE
A Garden of Peace

It is good to be alone in a garden at dawn or dark so that all its shy presences may haunt you and possess you in a reverie of suspended thought.

JAMES DOUGLAS
Down Shoe Lane

Dear, how charming it must be to walk out in one's own garden, and sit on a bench in the open air with a fountain and a leaden statue and a rolling stone and an arbour! Have a care of sore throat though, and the agoe.

THOMAS GRAY
in a letter to the Revd Norton Nicholls, 25 June 1769

I have banished all worldly care from my garden; it is a clean and open spot.

HSIEH LING-YIN, 410 AD

To a gardener there is nothing more exasperating than a hose that just isn't long enough.

CECIL ROBERTS
quoted in the *New York Times*, May 1951

The Persian king is zealously cared for, so that he may find gardens wherever he goes. Their name is Paradise, and they are full of all things fair and good that the earth can bring forth.

XENOPHON
on the gardens of Cyrus the Great

As for our love of gardens, it is the last refuge of art in the minds and souls of many Englishmen: if we did not care for gardens, I hardly know in what way of beauty we should care for.

SIR ARTHUR HELPS

Let each Gentleman ... reflect upon Horses and Dogs, Wine and Women, Cards and Folly, and then upon Planting. Will not the last engross his *Whole* Mind, and appear worthy of employing all his attention?

REVD WILLIAM HANBURY

If you want to be happy for a week, take a wife ... If you want to be happy all your life, make a garden.

CHINESE PROVERB

Though a life of retreat offers various joys,
None, I think, will compare with the time one employs
In the study of herbs, or in striving to gain
Some practical knowledge of nature's domain.
Get a garden! What kind you may get matters not.

ABBOT WALAFRID STRABO
Hortulus

A modest garden contains, for those who know how to look and to wait, more instruction than a library.

HENRI FRÉDÉRIC AMIEL
Private Journal

My garden will never make me famous,
I'm a horticultural ignoramus.

OGDEN NASH

Gardening is certainly the next amusement to reading, and as my sight will now permit me little of that, I am glad to form a taste that can give me so much employment, and be the plaything of my Age, now my pen and needle are almost useless to me.

LADY MARY WORTLEY MONTAGUE
in a letter to Lady Bute, 26 July 1748

A place where the mind goes to seed.

ANON.

If a man be weary with over-much study (for study is a weariness to the Flesh as Solomon by experience can tell you) there is no better place in the world to recreate himself than a Garden.

WILLIAM COLES
Art of Simpling, 1656

A morning-glory at my window satisfies me more than the metaphysics of books.

WALT WHITMAN
Song of Myself

Gardening has compensations out of all proportion to its goals. It is creation in the pure sense.

PHYLLIS McGINLEY
The Province of the Heart

The man who has planted a garden feels that he has done something for the good of the whole world.

CHARLES DUDLEY WARNER
My Summer in a Garden

Man's effort to improve his lot.

ANON.

I have often thought that if heaven had given me choice of my position and calling, it should have been on a rich spot of earth, well watered ... No occupation is so delightful to me as the culture of the earth.

THOMAS JEFFERSON

Soil sport.

ANON.

As gardening has been the inclination of kings and the choice of philosophers, so it has been the common favourite of public and private men; a pleasure of the greatest and the care of the meanest; and, indeed, an employment for which no man is too high nor too low.

SIR WILLIAM TEMPLE

When I go into my garden with a spade, and dig a bed, I feel such an exhilaration and health that I discover that I have been defrauding myself all this time in letting others do for me what I should have done with my own hands.

RALPH WALDO EMERSON
Man the Reformer

The best place to seek God ... You can dig for Him there.

GEORGE BERNARD SHAW
The Black Girl in Her Search for God

The best way to get real enjoyment out of the garden is to put on a wide straw hat, ... hold a little trowel in one hand and a cool drink in the other, and tell the man where to dig.

CHARLES BARR

Observing the ancient housekeeper wrestling with the plantlife in the garden, I occasionally point out a weed, and encourage her from the deckchair.

ARTHUR MARSHALL
quoted in *Radio Times*, July 1977

Our England is a garden, and such gardens are not made
By singing: – 'Oh, how beautiful!' and sitting in the shade.

RUDYARD KIPLING
'The Glory of the Garden'

'I also know,' said Candide, 'that we must cultivate our garden.'

'You are right,' said Pangloss; 'for when man was put in the garden of Eden, he was put there to work.'

VOLTAIRE
Candide

For the last forty years of my life I have broken my back, my fingernails, and sometimes my heart ...

VICTORIA SACKVILLE-WEST
on the making of Sissinghurst, in a letter to a gentleman who had accused her of being an armchair gardener.

A thing of beauty and a job forever.

ANON.

There is not amongst Men a more laborious Life than is that of a good Gard'ner's.

JOHN EVELYN
Kalendarium Hortense or *The Gard'ner's Almanac*, 1664

What a man needs in gardening is a cast-iron back with a hinge on it.

CHARLES DUDLEY WARNER
My Summer in a Garden

Something that is healthy exercise if one can straighten up afterwards.

ANON.

There is more pleasure in making a garden than in contemplating a paradise.

ANNE SCOTT-JAMES
Down to Earth

I will not enter upon any account of flowers, having only pleased myself with seeing or smelling them, and not troubled myself with the care, which is more the ladies' part than the men's.

SIR WILLIAM TEMPLE

Gentlewomen if the ground be not too wet may doe themselves much good by kneeling upon a Cushion and Weeding. And thus both sexes might divert themselves from Idlenesse and evill company.

WILLIAM COLES
Art of Simpling, 1656

The care of plants, such as needed peculiar care or skill to rear them, was the female province. Everyone in town or country had a garden. Into this garden no foot of man intruded after it was dug in the spring. I think I see yet what I so often beheld – a respectable mistress of a family going out to her garden, on an April morning, with her great calash, her little painted basket of seeds, and her rake over her shoulder, going to her gardens of labors.

MRS GRANT
Memoirs of an American Lady, 1808

If I could influence the fair sex, there is one thing to which I would draw their attention; and that is Horticulture ... I would recommend them, as far as convenient, to become Florists, as this delightful and healthy employment ... would entice them into the open air, stimulate them to exertion and draw them away from their sedentary modes of life, mewed up in close rooms, where they are confined like nuns.

THOMAS BEWICK
Memoir, 1822

My plan of Floriculture may be carried into effect by any lady who can command the services of an old man, a woman, or a stout boy.

LOUISA JOHNSON
Every Lady Her Own Flower Gardener, 1840

The Old Squire's Weeding Woman is our nursery-maid's aunt. She is not very old but she looks so, because she has lost her teeth, and is bent nearly double. She wears a large hood, and carries a big basket ...

JULIANA HORATIA EWING
Mary's Meadow, 1885

There came out of the house a lady with a handkerchief tied over her cap, and a pair of gardening gloves on her hands, wearing a gardening pocket like a toll-man's apron, and carrying a great knife. I knew her immediately to be Miss Betsey.

CHARLES DICKENS
David Copperfield

It is not graceful, and it makes one hot; but it is a blessed sort of work, and if Eve had had a spade in Paradise and known what to do with it, we should not have had all that sad business of the apple.

COUNTESS VON ARNIM
Elizabeth and Her German Garden

Pruning appears, at first sight, a most laborious and unfeminine occupation; and yet perhaps there is no operation of gardening which a lady may more easily accomplish. With the aid of a small, and almost elegant pair of pruning shears, which I procured from Mr Forrest, of Kensington Nursery, I have myself (though few women have less strength of wrist) divided branches that a strong man could scarcely cut through with a knife.

JANE LOUDON
Instructions in Gardening for Ladies, 1840

It must be confessed that digging appears, at first sight, a very laborious employment, and one peculiarly unfitted to small and delicately formed hands and feet; but, by a little attention to the principles of mechanics and the laws of motion, the labour may be much simplified and rendered comparatively easy …

JANE LOUDON
Instructions in Gardening for Ladies, 1840

The applicant for the gardener's place dined here and slept here while I was away. Frances was much struck by her. An *absolute* lady, *and* didn't flinch at manure stirring, or scullery drain, or anything! An unhappy marriage, and failing in market gardening has brought her to this.

LADY WOLSELEY
in a letter to her husband, 22 February 1903

Let us divide our labours, thou where choice
Leads thee, or where most needs, whether to wind
The Woodbine round this Arbour, or direct
The clasping Ivie where to climb, while I
In yonder Spring of Roses intermixt
With Myrtle, find what to redress till Noon.

JOHN MILTON
Eve gives directions to Adam in *Paradise Lost*

Is the fancy too far brought, that this love for gardens is a reminiscence haunting the race of that remote time when but two persons existed – a gardener named Adam, and a gardener's wife called Eve?

ALEXANDER SMITH
Dreamthorp, 1863

I have a cottage in Colebrook Row, Islington ... and behind is a spacious garden, ... to delight the heart of old Alcinous ... I am so taken up with pruning and gardening, quite a new sort of occupation to me ... I can now understand in what sense they speak of *Father Adam*. I recognize the paternity, while I watch my tulips.

CHARLES LAMB
in a letter to Bernard Barton, 2 September 1823

A garden was the primitive prison, till man with Promethean felicity and boldness, luckily sinned himself out of it.

CHARLES LAMB
in a letter to William Wordsworth, 22 January 1830

Gardening is an even more relentless and unending battle than the politics of Westminster.

JOHN BIFFEN
writing in *The Times*, December 1990

'*Beastly* garden!'

VICTORIA SACKVILLE-WEST
when things did not go according to plan

Last night, there came a frost, which has done great damage to my garden ... It is sad that Nature will play such tricks on us poor mortals, inviting us with sunny smiles to confide in her, and then, when we are entirely within her power, striking us to the heart.

NATHANIEL HAWTHORNE
The American Notebooks

How could sour cherries, or half-ripe strawberries, or wet rosebuds ... reward a man for the loss of the ease and the serene conscience of one who sings merrily in the streets, and cares not whether worms burrow, whether suns burn, whether birds steal, whether winds overturn, whether droughts destroy, whether floods drown, whether gardens flourish or not?

OLIVER BELL BUNCE
Bachelor Bluff

The principal value of a private garden ... is not to give the possessor vegetable and fruit (that can be better and cheaper done by the market-gardeners), but to teach him patience and philosophy, and the higher virtues – hope deferred and expectations blighted.

CHARLES DUDLEY WARNER
My Summer in a Garden

Seedsmen reckon that their stock in trade is not seeds at all ... it's optimism. That's what they're selling when you're seduced by that gorgeous picture on the front of the packet.

GEOFF HAMILTON
writing in *Radio Times*, November 1990

Gardening should really be done in blinders. Its distractions are tempting and persistent, and only by stern exercise of will do I ever finish one job without being lured off to another.

RICHARDSON WRIGHT
The Gardener's Bed-Book

It seems almost unnatural for a country clergyman to be without some love of flowers and gardens ... Yet it has its snares, of which the chief is that it may become too interesting and too absorbing. Its very innocence may help on and even conceal the snare.

CANON HENRY ELLACOMBE
In a Gloucestershire Garden, 1895

It is utterly forbidden to be half-hearted about gardening. You have got to love your garden whether you like it or not.

W.C. SELLAR & R.J. YEATMAN
Garden Rubbish

A garden is like those pernicious machineries which catch a man's coat-skirt or his hand, and draw in his arm, his leg and his whole body to irresistible destruction.

RALPH WALDO EMERSON
Conduct of Life: Wealth

The trouble with gardening is that it does not remain an avocation. It becomes an obsession.

PHYLLIS McGINLEY
The Province of the Heart

Man was made for better things than pruning his rose trees. The state of mind of the confirmed gardener seems to me as reprehensible as that of the confirmed alcoholic.

COLIN WILSON
A Book of Gardens

Old gardeners never die. They just spade away and then throw in the trowel.

HERBERT V. PROCHNOW, SR

Die when I may, I want it said by those who know me best, that I always plucked a thistle and planted a flower where I thought a flower would grow.

ABRAHAM LINCOLN

He that is a garden's friend,
Groweth calm and wise,
And after death shall rise and tend
A plot in paradise.

DOROTHY FRANCES GURNEY
'Garden Thoughts'

But though an old man, I am but a young gardener.

THOMAS JEFFERSON
in a letter to Charles Wilson Peale, 20 August 1811

All gardeners know better than other gardeners.

CHINESE PROVERB

They set great store by their gardens ... Their study and diligence herein cometh not only of pleasure, but also of certain strife and contention that is between street and street, concerning the trimming husbanding and furnishing of their gardens, every man for his own part.

SIR THOMAS MORE
Utopia

A man looked over the garden wall,
And said, 'Them hollyhocks is too tall.
Your flamin' roses got the blight,
Them beans got aphis, black as night ...'

H.L.V. FLETCHER
The Happy Gardener

You must not praise the elegance of an Englishman's house – though you may always be impressed by the garden.

GEORGE MIKES
How to Be an Alien

If the regular City man, who leaves Lloyd's at five o'clock, and drives home to Hackney, Clapton, Stamford-hill, or elsewhere, can be said to have any daily recreation beyond his dinner, it is in his garden. He never does anything to it with his own hands; but he takes great pride in it

notwithstanding; and if you are desirous of paying your addresses to the youngest daughter, be sure to be in raptures with every flower and shrub it contains.

CHARLES DICKENS
Sketches by Boz

Mr Collins invited them to take a stroll in the garden, which was large and well laid out, and to the cultivation of which he attended himself. To work in his garden was one of his most respectable pleasures ... Here, leading the way through every walk and cross walk, and scarcely allowing them an interval to utter the praises he asked for, every view was pointed out with a minuteness which left beauty entirely behind.

JANE AUSTEN
Pride and Prejudice

'My little plot,' said Miss Mapp. 'Very modest, as you see, three-quarters of an acre at the most, but well screened. My flower-beds: sweet roses, tortoise-shell butterflies. Rather a nice clematis. My Little Eden I call it ...'

E.F. BENSON
Mapp and Lucia

...The garden, Betsey! Let me take a look at it; it is delightful, such a beautiful collection of flowers all in bloom, so sweetly arranged with rows of orange-trees and china vases of flowers; why you would be in raptures!

ABIGAIL ADAMS
wife of the American ambassador to Paris in 1784, in a letter to her niece Betsey Cranch.

There is another and a very different class of men, whose recreation is their garden. An individual of this class, resides some short distance from town – say in the

Hampstead-road, or the Kilburn-road, or any other other road where the houses are small and neat, and have little slips of back garden.

In fine weather the old gentleman is almost constantly in the garden; and when it is too wet to go into it, he will look out of the window at it, by the hour together. He has always something to do there, and you will see him digging, and sweeping, and cutting, and planting, with manifest delight.

CHARLES DICKENS
Sketches by Boz

The patch of land he had made into a garden was famous in the town for the beauty of the flowers which he grew there ... By dint of hard work, constant care, and endless buckets of water, he had even become a creator, inventing certain tulips and dahlias which seemed to have been forgotten by nature.

VICTOR HUGO
Les Misérables

Van Baerle kept up his experiments, and the result was a succession of triumphs: in two years his beds became full of such marvellous tulips that no man, with the exception perhaps of Shakespeare or Rubens, could be said to have been so divinely creative.

ALEXANDRE DUMAS
La Tulipe Noire

The pleasures, the ecstasies, of the horticulturist are harmless and pure; a streak, a tint, a shade, become his triumph, ... secured alone by morning care, by evening caution, and the vigilance of days.

E. JESSE

I know nothing more misleading to the novice in gardening than Horticultural Shows ... the flowers themselves are lovely to look at; but neither the means employed, nor the end attained, is gardening.

ALFRED AUSTIN
The Garden That I Love, 1907

The chrysanthemum more almost than any other flower suffers from that megalomania which is the British gardener's sole ideal of beauty. All he cares for is to get a thing large; farewell colour, fragrance, elegance, so long as to have a vast draggled head that looks like a moulting mop dipped in stale lobster-sauce.

REGINALD FARRER
My Rock Garden, 1907

He found her in her garden, not one of the old-fashioned gardens, ... but in a first-rate gardener's garden, every plant forming part of a group, and not to be picked or touched on any account; all of them forced into bloom at the wrong time of the year, and each bearing a name that it was difficult to pronounce ... Helen was standing apparently absorbed in admiration of a *Lancifolium speciosum*, which she had been assured by her gardener was 'a better variety' of the *Lancifolium punctatum*.

EMILY EDEN
The Semi-Attached Couple

'I wouldn't want to make it look like a gardener's garden, all clipped an' spick an' span, would you?' he said. 'It's nicer like this with things runnin' wild, an' swingin' an' catchin' hold of each other.'

FRANCES HODGSON BURNETT
The Secret Garden

I think the true gardener is the reverent servant of Nature, not her truculent, wife-beating master.

REGINALD FARRER
In a Yorkshire Garden, 1909

I am a great one for flying in the face of nature, believing you can grow everything you want – even indoor plants outside.

SIR FREDERICK ASHTON
The Englishman's Garden

Some ladies asked me why their plant had died. They had got it from the very best place, and they were sure they had done their very best for it ... They had made a nice hole with their new trowel, and for its sole benefit they had bought a tin of Concentrated Fertilizer. This they had emptied into the hole, put in the plant, and covered it up and given it lots of water, and – it had died! And yet these were the best and kindest of women, who would never have dreamed of feeding a new-born infant on beefsteaks and raw brandy.

GERTRUDE JEKYLL
Wood and Garden

When you have done your best for a flower and it fails, you have some reason to be aggrieved.

FRANK SWINNERTON
Tokefield Papers

The truth is, I have a brown thumb. Every green thing I touch withers.

ROBERTSON DAVIES
The Table Talk of Samuel Marchbanks

Flowers have an expression of countenance as much as men or animals. Some seem to smile; some have a sad expression; some are pensive and diffident; others again are plain, honest and upright, like the broad-faced sunflower and the hollyhock.

HENRY WARD BEECHER
Star Papers: A Discourse of Flowers

...the rouged tulips, proud as beggars, condescendingly greeted me, the nervous sick lilies nodded with melancholy tenderness, the drunken red roses laughed at me from afar ...

HEINRICH HEINE
Reisebilder

As for rosemary,
I let it run all over my garden walls
Not only because my bees love it
But because 'tis the herb
Sacred to remembrance.

SIR THOMAS MORE

You have heard it said that flowers only flourish rightly in the garden of someone who loves them. I know you would like that to be true; and would think it a pleasant magic if you could flush your flowers into brighter bloom by a kind look upon them.

JOHN RUSKIN
Sesame and Lilies

As I work among my flowers, I find myself talking to them, reasoning and remonstrating with them, and adoring them as if they were human beings.

CELIA THAXTER
An Island Garden

To get the best results you must talk to your vegetables.

PRINCE CHARLES
quoted in the *Observer*, September 1986

The Weeding Woman told me – 'Aunt be mortal fond of her flowers, but she've no notions of gardening, not in the ways of a gentleman's garden. But she be after 'em all along, so well as the roomatiz in her back do let her, with an old shovel and a bit of stuff to keep the frost out, one time, and the old shovel and a bit of stuff to keep 'em moistened from the drought, another time; cuddling of 'em like Christians ... It zim as if her flowers be like new childern for her, spoilt childern, too.'

JULIANA HORATIA EWING
Mary's Meadow, 1885

She went forth among her fruits and flow'rs,
To visit how they prosper'd, bud and bloom
Her nursery: they at her coming sprung,
And touch'd by her fair tendance gladlier grew.

MILTON

She could grow them [flowers] anywhere, ... and they seemed to live longer for her. She grew them with rough, almost slap-dash love, but her hands possessed such an understanding of their needs they seemed to turn to her like another sun.

LAURIE LEE
Cider with Rosie

Perfumes are the feelings of flowers.

HEINRICH HEINE
The Hartz Journey

And because, the Breath of Flowers is farre Sweeter in the Aire (where it comes and Goes, like the Warbling of Musick) than in the hand, therfore nothing is more fit for that delight, than to know, what be the Flowers and Plants that doe best perfume the Aire ... That, which above all others, yeelds the Sweetest smell in the Aire is the Violet; specially the White-double-Violet, which comes twice a Yeare, about the middle of Aprill, and about Bartholomew-tide. Next to that is the Muske-Rose. Then the Strawberry-Leaves dying, which yeeld a most Excellent Cordiall smell.

FRANCIS BACON
Essays

Sweet is the garden, white with bloom,
Heavy with honey, drenched with scent.

KATHARINE TYNAN HINKSON
'Love Content', *A Lover's Breast-Knot*

They reached the flower-garden, and turned mechanically in at the gate that opened, through a high thick hedge, on an expanse of brilliant colour, which, after the green shades they had passed through, startled the eye like flames ... The flowers were glowing with their evening splendours; verbenas and heliotropes were sending up their finest incense. It seemed a gala where all was happiness and brilliancy, and misery could find no sympathy.

GEORGE ELIOT
Scenes of Clerical Life

... I know that if odour were visible, as colour is,
I'd see the summer garden in rainbow clouds.

ROBERT BRIDGES
'Testament of Beauty'

It was the moment between six and seven when every flower ... glows.

VIRGINIA WOOLF
Mrs Dalloway

Speak not – whisper not;
Here bloweth thyme and bergamot;
Softly on the evening hour,
Secret herbs their spices shower,
Dark-spiked rosemary and myrrh,
Lean-stalked, purple lavender ...

WALTER DE LA MARE
'The Sunken Garden'

No evening scents, I think, have the fascination of the delicate fragrance of the evening primroses, especially that of the commonest variety. Those pale moons irradiate the twilight with their sweet elusive perfumes.

ELEANOUR SINCLAIR ROHDE
The Scented Garden

A half-moon, dusky gold, was sinking behind the black sycamore at the end of the garden, making the sky dull purple with its glow. Nearer, a dim white fence of lilies went across the garden, and the air all round seemed to stir with scent ... He went across the beds of pinks, whose keen perfume came sharply across the rocking, heavy scent of the lilies, and stood alongside the white barrier of flowers. They flagged all loose, as if they were panting. The scent made him drunk.

D.H. LAWRENCE
Sons and Lovers

While such honey-dew fell, such silence reigned, such gloaming gathered, I felt as if I could haunt such shade for ever: but in threading the flower and fruit-parterres at the upper part of the inclosure, enticed there by the light the now-risen moon casts on this more open quarter, my step is stayed – not by sound, not by sight, but once more by a warning fragrance.

Sweet briar and southernwood, jasmine, pink, and rose, have long been yielding their evening sacrifice of incense: this new scent is neither of shrub nor flower; it is – I know it well – it is Mr Rochester's cigar.

CHARLOTTE BRONTË
Jane Eyre

Come into the garden, Maud.
I am here at the gate alone;
And the woodbine spices are wafted abroad,
And the musk of the rose is blown.

ALFRED, LORD TENNYSON
Maud

But nothing could exceed the freshness and beauty of the flowers, still loaded as they were with the moisture of the night, and this mysterious and shadowy hour of dawn, when they open, as if to ... shed those sweetest perfumes ...

GEORGE SAND
Consuelo

The green of the garden was greyed over with dew; indeed, all its colours were gone until the touch of sunrise. The air was still, and the tree-shapes crouched down upon themselves.

PHILIPPA PEARCE
Tom's Midnight Garden

The red flowers hang like a heavy mist,
The white flowers gleam like a fall of snow.
PO-CHU-I
translated by Arthur Waley, 9th century

Nothing so free and gracious, so lovely and wistful, nothing so richly coloured yet so ghost-like exists planted by the sons of man. It is a kind of paradise which has wandered down, a miraculously enchanted wilderness. Brilliant with azaleas, or magnolias, it centres round a pool of dreamy water, overhung by tall trunks, wanly festooned with the grey Florida moss. Beyond anything I have ever seen, it is other-worldly.
JOHN GALSWORTHY
describing the magnolia gardens near Charleston in South Carolina.

During the long rains in the Fifth Month, there is something very moving about a place with a pond. Between the dense irises, water-oats, and other plants one can see the green of the water; and the entire garden seems to be the same green colour.
THE PILLOW BOOK OF SEI SHONAGON
translated by Ivan Morris, 10th century

In every garden four things are necessary to be provided for – flowers, fruit, shade, and water; and whoever lays out a garden without all these must not pretend to any perfection. It ought to lie to the best parts of the house, or to those of the master's commonest use; so as to be but like one of the rooms out of which you step into another.
SIR WILLIAM TEMPLE

Large or small, the garden should look both orderly and rich. It should be well fenced from the outer world. It should by no means imitate either the wilfulness or the wildness of Nature, but should look like a thing never seen except near a house.

WILLIAM MORRIS
Hope and Fears for Art

I like the gardens with good bones and affirmed underlying structure ... well-marked paths, well-built walls, well-defined changes in level.

RUSSELL PAGE
The Education of a Gardener

Formality is often essential to the plan of a garden but never to the arrangement of its flowers or shrubs, and to array these in rigid lines, circles, or patterns can only be ugly wherever it may be.

WILLIAM ROBINSON
The English Flower Garden

Gardens ... should be like lovely, well-shaped girls: all curves, secret corners, unexpected deviations, seductive surprises and then still more curves.

H.E. BATES
A Love of Flowers

It is a common delusion among gardeners that their art is above the whims of fashion.

ANNE SCOTT-JAMES
Down to Earth

No pleasing intricacies intervene,
No artful wildness to perplex the scene;
Grove nods at grove, each alley has a brother,
And half the platform just reflects the other.
The suff'ring eye inverted nature sees,
Trees cut in statues, statues thick as trees
With here a fountain never to be play'd,
And there a summer house that knows no shade.

ALEXANDER POPE
Moral Essays

We saw the palace and Gardens of Versailles full of statues, vases, fountains, and colonnades. In all that belongs essentially to a garden they are extraordinarily deficient.

PERCY BYSSHE SHELLEY

When a Frenchman reads of the garden of Eden, I do not doubt but he concludes it was something approaching to that of Versailles, with clipt hedges, berceaus, and trellis-work.

HORACE WALPOLE
Essay on Modern Gardens

When we reached them we forgot all our troubles, so singular is the appearance of that called the Beautiful Island (Isola Bella). Imagine a quantity of arcades, formed in the centre of the lake, supporting a conical-shaped hill, cut in four sides, covered with thirty-six terraces, one over the other, nine on each side ... Each of these terraces is hung with palisades of jessamine, orange trees, or pomegranates, with pots of flowers placed on the ledge.

CHARLES DE BROSSES
describing the gardens of Isola Bella on Lake Maggiore.

I ascended terrace after terrace, robed by a thick underwood of bay and myrtle, above which rose several nodding towers, and a long sweep of venerable wall, almost entirely concealed by ivy. You would have been enraptured with the broad masses of shade and dusky alleys that opened as I advanced, with white statues of fauns and sylvans glimmering amongst them.

WILLIAM BECKFORD
describing the garden of Boboli, Florence, in *Italy, with Sketches of Spain and Portugal*

The water in the fountain was clearer and greener than an emerald; a maidenhair fern quivered, and a few rose petals floated, fallen from the bushes above.

GABRIELE D'ANNUNZIO
Il Piacere

Of course you saw the Villa d'Este Gardens,'
Writes one of my Italianistic friends.
Of course, of course; I saw them in October,
Spired with pinaceous ornamental gloom
Of that arboreal elegy the cypress.

SIEGFRIED SASSOON

I think no English garden is as lovely as a foreign one. These gardens are created for rest in cool surroundings, for idleness and sauntering and imaginative thought, ... but never for a show of tinkling tea-cups and hoarse cries of 'Love-all'.

OSBERT SITWELL

He had been visiting a friend in a neighbouring county, and that friend having recently had his grounds laid out by an improver, Mr Rushworth was returned with his head full of the subject, and very eager to be improving his own place in the same way ...

'I must try to do something with it,' said Mr Rushworth, 'but I do not know what. I hope I shall have some good friend to help me.'

'Your best friend upon such an occasion,' said Miss Bertram, calmly, 'would be Mr Repton, I imagine.'

'That is what I was thinking of. As he has done so well by Smith, I think I had better have him at once. His terms are five guineas a day.'

JANE AUSTEN
Mansfield Park

The perfection of landscape gardening consists in the four following requisites: *First* it must display the natural beauties, and hide the natural defects of every situation. *Secondly* it should give the appearance of extent and freedom, by carefully disguising or hiding the boundary. *Thirdly* it must studiously conceal every inference of art, however expensive, by which the natural scenery is improved ... *Fourthly* all objects of mere convenience or comfort, if incapable of being made ornamental ... must be removed or concealed.

HUMPHREY REPTON
Theory and Practice of Landscape Gardening

A skilful painter hardly does more for his blank sheet of canvass, than the landscape-gardener ... has done for the monotonous surface of Blenheim; ... putting in beauty as often as there was a niche for it; opening vistas to every point that deserved to be seen ... – and then, to be sure, the lapse of a century has softened the harsh outline of man's labors ... Positively, the garden of Eden cannot have been more beautiful than this private garden of Blenheim.

NATHANIEL HAWTHORNE
Our Old Home, 1863

The taste of the English in the cultivation of land, and in what is called landscape gardening, is unrivalled. They have studied nature intently, and discover an exquisite sense of her beautiful forms and harmonious combinations. Those charms which in other countries she lavishes in wild solitudes are here assembled round the haunts of domestic life.

WASHINGTON IRVING

Of the many gardens I have seen, very few gave me the pleasure of Powis ...The flower garden is beautiful, partly owing to its position, which is that of a true terrace garden – ie, the ground falls so steeply, that terracing is necessary. These terraces were wreathed with clematis and beautiful with shrub, and flower, and life, a picture of what a flower garden should be ... A happy idea is carried out in regard to colours by the three terraces having each its predominating colour – viz, the lowest white, the middle yellow, and the highest purple; not that other colours are excluded, but these prevailing tones are maintained.

WILLIAM ROBINSON
The English Flower Garden

Our England is a garden that is full of stately views,
Of borders, beds and shrubberies and lawns and avenues,
With statues on the terraces and peacocks strutting by;
But the Glory of the Garden lies in more than meets the
eye.

For where the old thick laurels grow, along the thin red
  wall,
You find the tool- and potting-sheds which are the heart
  of all;
The cold-frames and the hot-houses, the dung-pits and
  the tanks,
The rollers, carts and drain-pipes, with the barrows and
  the planks.

RUDYARD KIPLING
'The Glory of the Garden'

I have seen one clambering rose, one lingering hollyhock, glorify a cottage home, arrest one's step, and prolong one's meditations, more than all the terraces of Chatsworth.

ALFRED AUSTIN

Some of these cottages in summer-time really approach something of that Arcadian beauty which is supposed to prevail in the country ... Near the door there are almost always a few cabbage-rose trees, and under the windows grow wall-flowers and hollyhocks, sweet peas, columbine and sometimes the graceful lilies of the valley. The garden stretches in a long strip from the door, one mass of green. It is enclosed by thick hedges, over which the dog-rose grows, and the wild convolvulus will blossom in the autumn. Trees fill up every available space and corner – apple trees, pear trees, damsons, plums, bullaces – all varieties.

RICHARD JEFFERIES

...the latticed bedroom windows standing open to let in the sweet-smelling air, and the ragged old rooks'-nests still dangling in the elm-trees at the bottom of the front garden. Now I am in the garden at the back ... – a very preserve of butterflies, as I remember it, with a high fence and a gate and padlock; where the fruit clusters on the trees, riper and richer than fruit has ever been since, in any other garden, and where my mother gathers some in a basket, while I stand by, bolting furtive gooseberries, and trying to look unmoved.

CHARLES DICKENS
David Copperfield

A little garden not too fine,
Enclosed with painted pales.
And woodbines round the cot to twine,
Pin to the wall with nails.

Let hazels grow, and spindling sedge,
Bent bowering overhead;
Dig 'old man's beard' from woodland hedge
To twine a summer shade

JOHN CLARE

The only garden flowers I care for are the quite old fashioned roses, sunflowers, hollyhocks, lilies, and so on, and these I like to see growing as much as possible as if they were wild. Trim and symmetrical beds are my abhorrence, and most of the flowers which are put into them – hybrids with some grotesque name – Jonesia, Snooksia – hurt my eyes. On the other hand, a garden is a garden, and I would not try to introduce into it the flowers which are my solace in lanes and fields.

GEORGE GISSING
The Private Papers of Henry Ryecroft

I have a garden of my own,
But so with roses overgrown
And lilies, that you would it guess
To be a little wilderness.

ANDREW MARVELL
'The Nymph Complaining for the Death of Her Faun'

As is the garden such is the gardener.

HEBREW PROVERB

As spring came on ... the garden had to be put in order, and each sister had a quarter of the little plot to do what she liked with. Hannah used to say, 'I'd know which each of them gardens belonged to, ef I see 'em in Chiny.'

LOUISA M. ALCOTT
Little Women

The garden was a wide enclosure, surrounded with walls so high as to exclude every glimpse of prospect; a covered verandah ran down one side, and broad walks bordered a middle space divided into scores of little beds: these beds were assigned as gardens for the pupils to cultivate, and each bed had an owner. When full of flowers they would doubtless look pretty.

CHARLOTTE BRONTË
Jane Eyre

My gardens sweet, enclosed with walles strong,
Enbanked with benches to sytt and take my rest
The Knotts so enknotted, it cannot be exprest,
With arbors and alys so plesaunt and so dulce,
The pestylent ayers with flauors to repulse.

GEORGE CAVENDISH
writing about the gardens at Hampton Court.

The beds were bordered with little low hedges of box, smooth as green walls, cut into trim shapes like the hedge. There were bushes of Lad's-Love which sent out their rich fragrance, and lanes of lavender, and clumps of spraying rosemary ...

ALISON UTTLEY
description of an Elizabethan garden in *A Traveller in Time*

My gardens are in a window like those of a lodger up three pairs of stairs in Petticoat Lane or Camomile Street, and they go to bed regularly under the same roof as I do.

THOMAS GRAY
in a letter to the Revd Norton Nicholls, 25 June 1769

They called him the 'garden sorcerer' ... The old man had seen half the world's gardens, but preferred the dark corners of small courtyards or balconies where a few straggling geraniums might be growing.

GIOVANNI ARPINO
Il Mago dei giardini

The Island of Manhattan ... is set with cheerful habitations, with well-stocked gardens, and neat enclosures, while the heights, and many of the lower grounds, contain a rich display of gentlemen's country seats connected with a great variety of handsome appendages [gardens].

REVD TIMOTHY DWIGHT
Travels in New York and New England, 1791

Sun and air are the lungs and hearts of flowers. A lady will be rewarded for her trouble in making her parterre in the country; but in large towns, under the influence of coal smoke, shade and gloom, her lot will be constant disappointment. She can only hope to keep a few consumptive geraniums languishing through the summer months, to die in October, and show the desolating view of rows of pots containing blackened and dusty stems.

LOUISA JOHNSON
Every Lady Her Own Flower Gardener, 1840

Green are the lawns of country places, and the blooms are abundant. Yet we've wondered often if the dweller in peaceful blooming suburb experiences the grand passion that fires the man with a city back-garden.

E. B. WHITE
Every Day Is Saturday

The original Garden of Eden could not have had such turf as one sees in England.

CHARLES DUDLEY WARNER
My Summer in a Garden

The glory of the Small House at Allington certainly consists in its lawn, which is as smooth, as level, and as much like velvet as grass has ever yet been made to look.

ANTHONY TROLLOPE
The Small House at Allington

There were the smoothest lawns in the world stretching down to the edge of the liquid slowness and making, where the water touched them, a line as even as the rim of a champagne glass ... The place was a garden of delight.

HENRY JAMES

...Past the lime, the lawn,
Which, after sweeping broadly round the house,
Went trickling through the shrubberies in a stream
Of tender turf, and wore and lost itself
Among the acacias ...

ELIZABETH BARRETT BROWNING
Aurora Leigh

Nothing refreshes the sight so much as fine short grass. One must clear the space destined for a pleasure garden of all roots, and this can hardly be achieved unless the roots are dug out, the surface is levelled as much as possible, and boiling water is poured over the surface, so that the remaining roots and seeds which lie in the ground are destroyed and cannot germinate ... The ground must then be covered with turves cut from good grass, and beaten down with wooden mallets, and stamped down well with the feet until they are hardly able to be seen. Then little by little the grass pushes through like fine hair, and covers the surface like a fine cloth.

ALBERTUS MAGNUS
De Vegetabilibus, 13th century

The kind of grass I've got in the garden lies down under the mower, and pops up again as soon as it's passed.

BASIL BOOTHROYD

A garden without trees scarcely deserves to be called a garden.

CANON HENRY ELLACOMBE
In a Gloucestershire Garden, 1895

For the ordinary bedding-out of ordinary gardens I have a real contempt. It is at once gaudy and monotonous. A garden is left bare for eight months in the year, that for the four hottest months there shall be a blaze of the hottest colours. The same combination of the same flowers appear wherever you go – Calceolarias, Verbenas, and Zonal Pelargoniums, with a border of Pyrethrums or Cerastiums; and that is about all.

HENRY A. BRIGHT
A Year in a Lancashire Garden, 1879

The garden which lay around it would be a lady watercolourist's heaven, herbaceous borders, rockeries, and water-gardens were carried to a perfection of vulgarity, and flaunted a riot of huge and hideous flowers.

NANCY MITFORD
Love in a Cold Climate

'One likes a mosaic pavement to look like a garden,' said Euphrosyne, 'but not a garden like a mosaic pavement.'

BENJAMIN DISRAELI
Lothair

Bedding, though it is gardening of the least poetical or imaginative kind, can be done badly or beautifully. In the *parterre* of the formal garden it is absolutely in place, and brilliantly beautiful pictures can be made by a wise choice of colouring.

GERTRUDE JEKYLL
Wood and Garden

There is nothing much more difficult to do in outdoor gardening than to plant a mixed border well, and to keep it in beauty through the summer.

GERTRUDE JEKYLL
Wood and Garden

I am one, you must know, who am looked upon as a humorist in gardening. I have several acres about my house, which I call my garden, and which a skilful gardener would not know what to call. It is a confusion of kitchen and parterre, orchard and flower garden, which lie so mixt and interwoven with one another, that if a foreigner who had seen nothing of our country should be conveyed into my garden at his first landing, he would look upon it as a natural wilderness.

JOSEPH ADDISON
The Spectator

Adam walked ... to the little wooden gate leading into the garden – once the well-tended kitchen-garden of a manor-house; now ... a true farmhouse garden, with hardy perennial flowers, unpruned fruit-trees, and kitchen vegetables growing together in careless, half-neglected abundance ... There were the tall hollyhocks beginning to flower, and dazzle the eye with their pink, white, and yellows; there were the syringas and Gueldres roses, all large and disorderly for want of trimming; there were leafy walls of scarlet beans and late peas.

GEORGE ELIOT
Adam Bede

Here was a variety of fruit and everything useful for the kitchen, which was abundantly sufficient to catch the admiration of Adams, who told the gentleman he had certainly a good gardener. Sir, answered he, that gardener is now before you; whatever you see here is the work solely of my own hands. Whilst I am providing necessaries for my table, I likewise procure myself an appetite for them.

HENRY FIELDING
Joseph Andrews

In order to live off a garden, you practically have to live in it.

FRANK McKINNEY HUBBARD

It is most miserable taste to seek to poke away the kitchen-garden, in order to get it out of sight. If well managed, nothing is more beautiful than the kitchen-garden: the earliest blossoms come there: we shall in vain seek for flowering shrubs ... to equal the peaches, nectarines, apricots, and plums.

WILLIAM COBBETT
The English Gardener

...rich chocolate earth studded emerald green, frothed with the white of cauliflowers, jewelled with the purple globes of eggplant and the scarlet wealth of tomatoes.

DORIS LESSING
The Habit of Loving

...the vegetable plot, melancholy now with rimed bolted cabbage stalks and blackened stands of beans. The people of Innstead concealed their vegetable gardens, preferring to contemplate in season the useless glories of aster and delphinium, petunia and pelargonium, lobelia, lupin, chrysanthemum and mesembryanthemum.

ALICE THOMAS ELLIS
The Birds of the Air

On one side is a gloomy garden, with an old man digging in it, laid out in straight dark beds of vegetables, potatoes, cabbages, onions, beans, all earthy and mouldy as a newly-dug grave. Not a flower or flowering shrub! Not a rose-tree or currant-bush! Nothing but for sober, melancholy use. Oh, how different from the long irregular slips of the cottage-gardens, with their gay bunches of polyanthuses and crocuses, their wallflowers sending sweet odours through the narrow casement, and their gooseberry-trees bursting into a brilliancy of leaf ...

MARY MITFORD
Our Village

The garden was divided into four square beds bordered with box. Madame Magloire grew vegetables in three of them, while in the fourth, the bishop had planted flowers; there were also a few fruit trees. She had once said to him, with gentle malice, 'Your Grace always makes the most of things, yet this bed produces nothing. Salads would be more useful than bouquets.' 'Madame Magloire,' replied the bishop, 'you are misguided. The beautiful is as useful as the useful – more so, perhaps ...'

VICTOR HUGO
Les Misérables

The garden was not very productive, save of weeds, and perhaps, tremendous lank artichokes or swollen marrows. But at the bottom, ... there was a plum-tree which had been crucified to the wall, and which had broken away and leaned forward from bondage. Now under the boughs were hidden great mist-bloomed, crimson treasures, splendid globes. I shook the old ragged trunk, ... and the treasures fell heavily, thudding down among the immense rhubarb leaves below.

D.H. LAWRENCE

Tall thriving trees confess the fruitful mould;
The redd'ning apple ripens here to gold;
Here the blue fig with luscious juice o'erflows,
With deeper red the full pomegranate glows:
The branch here bends beneath the weighty pear,
And verdant olives flourish round the year.
The balmy spirit of the western gale,
Eternal breathes on fruits untaught to fail:
Each dropping pear a following pear supplies,
On apples apples, figs on figs arise ...

HOMER
description of the garden of Alcinous, *The Odyssey*,
Alexander Pope's translation

The principal Art of a Gardiner consists in pruning: for which observe these Rules: Learn first to know the bearing buds from the leafe buds, and those which will be fruite-buds next yeare; sparing all the fruite budds of standard Apples, Peares & wall-fruite with discretion. Cut allwayes above the bud slanting that the water may passe off, and let the kniffe be very sharp, that you leave no raggs.

JOHN EVELYN
Directions for the Gardiner at Says-Court

They went from bush to bush and from tree to tree. He was very strong and clever with his knife and knew how to cut the dry and dead wood away, and could tell when an unpromising bough or twig had still green life in it.

FRANCES HODGSON BURNETT
The Secret Garden

The hook she bore
To lop the growth of the luxuriant year,
To decent form the lawless shoots to bring,
And teach th'obedient branches where to spring.

ALEXANDER POPE

The first day I turned a drunken gardener (as he let in the serpent) into my Eden, and he laid about him, lopping off some choice boughs, etc, which hung over a neighbour's garden, and in his blind zeal laid waste a shade, which had sheltered their window from the gaze of passers-by. The old gentlewoman (fury made her not handsome) could scarcely be reconciled by all my fine words. There was no buttering her parsnips. She talked of the law.

CHARLES LAMB
in a letter to Bernard Barton, 2 September 1823

Most people who possess anything like an acre, or half of it, contribute weekly to the support of a gentleman known as Jobbing Gardener. You are warned of the danger that he may prove to be Garden Pest no 1.

C.E. LUCAS-PHILLIPS
The New Small Garden

My father ... strode about sowing death and destruction. Shears in hand he took to pruning. The havoc was terrible, and when we came back at night, what that morning had been a shrubbery was now reduced to a sort of skeleton espalier.

GEORGES DUHAMEL
In Sight of the Promised Land

His greatest passion is for transplanting. Everything we possess he moves from one end of the garden to another, to produce better effects. Roses take place of jessamines, jessamines of honeysuckles, and honeysuckles of lilacs, till they have all danced round as far as the space allows.

FANNY BURNEY
about the gardening efforts of her husband, M. d'Arblay, in a letter to her father, 1794.

Never fail, as you go by, to record what bush is to be moved, and which retained, and which is pretty, and which, on consideration, is held unworthy of too prominent a place.

REGINALD FARRER
In a Yorkshire Garden, 1909

Never, never, never again will I attempt the bulbous irises.

REGINALD FARRER
In a Yorkshire Garden, 1909

Muscari, she wrote. They had not really liked being under the cedar; it was far too dry for them. If she wanted drifts of blue under the cedar, she would have to make do with bluebells.

ELIZABETH JANE HOWARD
Odd Girl Out

Neither graft, set, sow, or plant anything that day whereon there happeneth an Eclipse either of Sun or Moon, or when the Moon is afflicted by either of the infortunes Saturn or Mars.

REVD SAMUEL GILBERT
Florists Vade Mecum, 1683

In Lincolnshire, to test whether the soil was in the right condition for sowing barley, farmers used to take off their trousers and sit on the ground: if it was comfortable for them it would be comfortable for the barley.

MAUREEN AND BRIDGET BOLAND
Old Wives' Lore for Gardeners

The second article which I pronounce to be indispensable is a pair of Indian rubber shoes, or the wooden high-heeled shoes called 'sabots' by the French. In these protections, a lady may indulge her passion for flowers at all seasons, without risk of rheumatism or chills.

LOUISA JOHNSON
Every Lady Her Own Flower Gardener, 1840

Perhaps the most useful covering for the feet is a kind of clog and gaiter combined ... She should also have a pair of stiff thick leathern gloves, or gauntlets, to protect her hands, not only from the handle of the spade, but from the stones, weeds etc which she may turn over with the earth.

JANE LOUDON
Instructions in Gardening for Ladies, 1840

They considered keeping the soil constantly stirred about the roots of growing things the secret of success and used the Dutch hoe a good deal for this purpose. The process was called 'tickling' – 'Tickle up old Mother Earth and make her bear!'

FLORA THOMPSON
Lark Rise to Candleford

Authorities differ as to the best way of hoeing up a garden ... All agree that it is impossible to avoid walking for a week afterwards as if you were imitating an old waiter with lumbago.

ROBERT BENCHLEY
Inside Benchley

I am told that abundant and rank weeds are signs of a rich soil; but I have noticed that a thin, poor soil grows little but weeds.

CHARLES DUDLEY WARNER
My Summer in a Garden

I will go root away
The noisome weeds, that without profit suck
The soil's fertility from wholesome flowers.

SHAKESPEARE
Richard II

'Fine for the flowers
The lovely showers,'
Is pretty reading,
But, oh, the weeding!
FRANKLIN PIERCE ADAMS

...Having been left so many years, untilled and untrimmed, abandoned to the weeds and the grass, to the frost and the wind, the rain and the drought, it presented a very singular appearance indeed. The close green walls of privet, that had bordered the principal walk, were two-thirds withered away, and the rest grown beyond all reasonable bounds; the old boxwood swan ... had lost its neck and half its body.
ANNE BRONTË
The Tenant of Wildfell Hall

Near yonder copse, where once the garden smil'd,
And still where many a garden flower grows wild ...
OLIVER GOLDSMITH
The Deserted Village

It was the sweetest, most mysterious-looking place anyone could imagine. The high walls which shut it in were covered with the leafless stems of climbing roses, which were so thick that they were matted together ... There were numbers of standard roses which had so spread their branches that they were like little trees. There were other trees in the garden, and one of the things which made the place look strangest and loveliest was that climbing roses had run all over them and swung down long tendrils which made light swaying curtains.
FRANCES HODGSON BURNETT
The Secret Garden

One of the most delightful things about a garden is the anticipation it provides.

W.E. JOHNS
The Passing Show

Ten thousand dangers lie in wait ...
...Heat and cold, and wind, and steam,
Moisture and drought, mice, worms, and swarming flies,
Minute as dust, and numberless, oft work
Dire disappointment that admits no cure,
And which no care can obviate.

WILLIAM COWPER
'The Garden'

On every stem, on every leaf, ...and at the root of everything that grew, was a professional specialist in the shape of grub, caterpillar, aphis, or other expert, whose business it was to devour that particular part.

OLIVER WENDELL HOLMES

The morning sunshine ... fell on the baggy trousers-seat of Angus McAllister, head gardener to the ninth Earl of Emsworth, as he bent with dour Scottish determination to pluck a slug from its reverie beneath the leaf of a lettuce.

P.G. WODEHOUSE
Blandings Castle

These are most anxious times on account of the slugs. Now, every morning when I rise I go at once into the garden at four o'clock and make a business of slaughtering them till half past five, when I stop for breakfast.

CELIA THAXTER
An Island Garden, 1894

We have descended into the garden and caught three hundred slugs. How I love the mixture of the beautiful and the squalid in gardening. It makes it so lifelike.

EVELYN UNDERHILL
Letters

Dogs and Cats ought not to be suffer'd in a Flower Garden. Your Dogs do, by their continual leaping, leave ugly Marks or Impressions upon the Surface of the Ground – and the Cats scattering their Ordure all about, and then scraping the Earth to cover it, grub up many Plants.

The Compleat Florist, 1706

One evening Boxtel tied two cats together by a back paw, with a string ten feet long, and threw them from the top of the wall into the middle of the main flower bed in Van Baerle's garden, which contained some of his new creations ... As they fell on the bed the bewildered animals

tried to get away, making the string go taut; and then, as they struggled, they scrabbled all over the bed with frightful miauwls, while the string decapitated the flowers.

ALEXANDRE DUMAS
a jealous neighbour sets out to destroy Van Baerle's prize tulips, *La Tulipe Noire*

My great apricot-tree appeared in the morning to have been robbed of some of its ripe fruit by a dog that had stood on his hind legs, and eaten-off some of the lower apricots, several of which were gnawn, and left on the ground, with some shoots of the tree. On the border were many fresh prints of a dogs feet.

GILBERT WHITE
The Naturalist's Journal

The mice have played mischief with the Broad-beans in the Orchard; all about lie the withered tops of the plantlings destroyed by them, their habit being to dig up the seed and devour it. In despair, ...I procured a tinful of paraffin and soaked the seed, in the hope that this oil flavouring will disgust these thieves.

H. RIDER HAGGARD
A Gardener's Year

M. d'Arblay has worked most laboriously in his garden, but his misfortunes there, during our absence, might melt a heart of stone. The horses of our neighbouring farmer broke through our hedges, and have made a kind of bog of our meadow, by scampering in it during the wet; the sheep followed, who have eaten up all our greens, every sprout and cabbage and lettuce destined for the winter, while the horses dug up our turnips and carrots; and the swine, pursuing such examples, have trod down all the young plants, besides devouring whatever the others left of vegetables.

FANNY BURNEY
about the gardening trials of her husband in a letter to her father, 1794

He is a bad gardener whose garden is kept only for himself. Paradise was not made for Adam only, but for 'every beast of the field and every fowl of the air ...' ... Even our greatest enemies, the slugs, snails, and mice, which may be caught and killed without mercy, add to the interest of our garden.

CANON HENRY ELLACOMBE
In a Gloucestershire Garden, 1895

I value my garden more for being full of blackbirds than of cherries, and very frankly give them fruit for their songs.

JOSEPH ADDISON
The Spectator, 1712

Though they [blackbirds] will strip the strawberry bed and raspberry rows I delight to have them in my garden. Their warbling song is more agreeable to my ear than the singing of the nightingale.

D.J. WATKINS-PITCHFORD ('BB')
The Naturalist's Bedside Book

What would become of the garden if the gardener treated all the weeds and slugs and birds and trespassers as he would like to be treated?

T.E. HUXLEY

...plants pecked to death by sparrows, dug up, trodden on, sat on or stolen, or simply annihilated by a blast of animal urine or overwhelmed by a cloaking turd ...

GERMAINE GREEN writing as Rose Blight
The Revolting Garden

Well must the ground be digg'd, and better dress'd,
New soil to make, and meliorate the rest.

JOHN DRYDEN

Doves dung is ye best, because the same possesseth a mightie hoteness.

The dung also of the hen and other foules greatly commended for the sournesse, except ye dung of geese, ducks, and other waterfoules.

A commendation next is attributed to the Asses dung, in that the same beast for his leisurely eating, digesteth easier, and causeth the better dung.

The third in place is the Goates dung, after this both ye Oxe and Cow dung; next the Swines dung ...

The dung which men make ... is greatly mislyked, for that by nature it is hoter, and burneth the seedes sowne in that earth.

THOMAS HILL
The Gardener's Labyrinth, 1586

Pidgeons and sheepes dung infused in Water is excellent for Oranges, choice greenes, and indeed any Fruite.

The scouring of muddy-ponds, and where cattell drinke and stand, is good for all plants.

The scouring of privies and sinkes so well dried and made sweete, well mixed with fresh earth so as to retain no heady scent, is above all other excellent for Oranges and the like choice fruits.

JOHN EVELYN
Directions to the Gardiner at Says-Court

Humane Ordure has, for a long time, been thought unfit for Land, as being too fiery; but this Heat may easily be allay'd with Straw, Fern, Earth, or any Vegetables, to give it a Fermentation, and then it is the Greatest Improver of any Dung whatsoever.

THOMAS TUSSER
Five Hundred Points of Good Husbandry, 1573

To dig and delve in nice clean dirt
Can do a mortal little hurt.

JOHN KENDRICK BANGS
'Gardening'

Returning on a summer's afternoon from a parochial walk, I inferred from wheel-tracks on my carriage-drive that callers had been and gone. I expected to find cards in the hall, and

I saw that the horses had kindly left theirs on the gravel ... I looked around and listened; no sight, no sound, of humanity. I fetched the largest fire-shovel I could find, and was carrying it bountifully laden through an archway cut in a high hedge of yews ... when I suddenly confronted three ladies ...

REVD SAMUEL REYNOLDS HOLE, Dean of Rochester
A Book About Roses, 1869

A real gardener is not a man who cultivates flowers; he is a man who cultivates the soil ... If he came into the Garden of Eden he would sniff excitedly and say: 'Good Lord, what humus!'

KAREL ČAPEK
The Gardener's Year

January 1904 Now in the first days of the new year ... I gather this morning a white Rosebud and a single flower of Anemone that is whiter yet. To me the one is as a ghost from the grave of dead, forgotten summer, and the other a spirit of the Spring, breathing that eternal promise ...

H. RIDER HAGGARD
A Gardener's Year

The garden is never dead; growth is always going on, and growth that can be seen, and seen with delight.

CANON HENRY ELLACOMBE
In My Vicarage Garden, 1902

5 January I never saw such Christmas Roses as I have just now. Clustering beneath their dark serrated leaves rise masses of bloom ... the bud often tinged with a faint pink colour, the blossom a snowy white guarding a centre of yellow stamens.

HENRY BRIGHT
A Year in a Lancashire Garden, 1901

...that beautiful half-blown Christmas rose, just peeping from the snow that had hitherto, no doubt, defended it from the frost, and was now melting away in the sun ...

ANNE BRONTË
The Tenant of Wildfell Hall

January may be called the digging month, as almost the only gardening operation that can be performed in it is digging, or rather trenching the ground.

JANE LOUDON
Instructions in Gardening for Ladies, 1840

January Pray for snow to make digging impossible.

SPIKE HUGHES
The Coarse Gardener's Calendar

The Snowdrop gives me chilblains, only to look at it – and the very sight of a Snowdrop will always make me hurry to the fireside. Was there ever such an icy, inhuman, bloodless flower, crystallised winter in three gleaming petals and a green-flecked cup?

REGINALD FARRER
In a Yorkshire Garden, 1909

20 January The first Aconite? Does any flower in summer give the same pleasure? The blue-green blades of the Daffodils and Jonquils are firmly and strongly pushing through the cold brown earth; nothing in all the year gives such a sense of power and joy.

MRS C.W. EARLE
Pot-Pourri from a Surrey Garden, 1897

4 February 1684 I went to Says-Court to see how the frost and rigorous weather had dealt with my garden, where I found many of the greens and rare plants utterly destroyed; the oranges and myrtles very sick, the rosemary and laurel dead to all appearance.

JOHN EVELYN
Diary

February 1903 Another week has gone by, the weather on February 16th remaining of the same extraordinary mild and rainless character. Indeed, gardeners about here say that they can remember no such season, and that the fruit trees are fuller of sap than they have ever seen them at this time of year ... All this is of very evil omen.

H. RIDER HAGGARD
A Gardener's Year

February If the weather be mild in this month, there is a great deal of business to be done in the Kitchen Garden, which, if omitted, will be of bad consequence, most of the principal crops being now to be sown or planted; which if done later in the year, do seldom succeed so well.

PHILIP MILLER
The Gardeners Kalendar, 1732

...a lovely clump of dwarf iris, whose name I believe to be Iris *histrio*, though I am not quite sure, deep blue, freckled with brilliant gold spots, are sunning themselves with the utmost self-complacency.

ALFRED AUSTIN
The Garden That I Love, 1907

The vernal Crocus or Saffron flowers of the Spring, white, purple, yellow and stript, some Dens Caninus or Dogges teeth, and some of the small early Leucojum or Bulbous violet, all planted in some proportion as neare unto one another as is fit for them will give such a grace to the Garden, that the place will seem like a piece of tapestry of many glorious colours.

JOHN PARKINSON
Paradisi in sole, Paradisus terrestris, 1629

Each spring ... a gardening instinct, sure as the sap rising in the trees, stirs within us. We look about and decide to tame another little bit of ground.

LEWIS GANNETT
Crown Hill

March Bestir your self now in grafting; and early on good Plumstocks, graft Apricocks, Nectarines and Peeches. Some may miss, but never all yet with me.

REVD SAMUEL GILBERT
The Florist's Vade-Mecum, 1683

In March and in Aprill, from morning to night:
in sowing and setting, good huswives delight.

THOMAS TUSSER
Five Hundred Points of Good Husbandry, 1573

The seed, selected wisely, plump, and smooth,
And glossy, he commits to pots of size
Diminutive, well fill'd with well-prepar'd
And fruitful soil ...
Then rise the tender germs, upstarting quick,
And spreading wide their spongy lobes; at first
Pale, wan, and livid; but assuming soon,
If fann'd by balmy and nutritious air,
Strain'd through the friendly mats, a vivid green.

WILLIAM COWPER
'The Garden'

30 March 1876 A lovely warm sunny morning, the purple plumes of the silver birch fast thickening with buds waved and swayed gently in the soft spring air against the deep cloudless blue sky. The apricot blossoms were blowing and under the silver weeping birch the daffodils were dancing and nodding their golden heads in the morning wind and sunshine.

REVD FRANCIS KILVERT
Diary

In an old Rectory Garden, neglected and weedy but beautiful in its negligence, I found the daffodils in full bloom, shaking their golden heads over an embroidery of crocus and primrose, or flaming like torches down some dark and grass-grown alley.

GEORGE MILNER
Country Pleasures

If you really want your heart to dance with the daffodils ... you must put in at least six times as many daffodils as you expect to see, and then – ah then, when April comes, your heart will dance, lightly enough!

BEVERLEY NICHOLS
Down the Garden Path

Welcome, sweet April! thou gentle Midwife of May's Pride and the Earth's green Livery. Sow your Garden Seeds and Plant Herbs, finish your grafting on the Stock. Open your Hives and give your Bees free Liberty to look into the Garden.

M. STEVENSON
17th century

20 April 1903 During the last nine days ... we have experienced quite the bitterest weather that I ever remember at this time of year ... It is said that no such cold has been known at this season since Easter Day, 1816 ... The effects upon vegetation are lamentable.

H. RIDER HAGGARD
A Gardener's Year

How beautiful a garden is when all the fruit-trees are in bloom, and how various that bloom is! Each Pear-tree bears a different blossom from its neighbour, and the handsomest of all, in size and shape of flower and form of cluster, is the Jargonelle. But no Pear-blossom can compare with the beauty of blossom on the Apple-trees; and of all Apple-trees the Pomeroy is most beautiful, when every bough is laden with clusters of deep-red buds, which shade off into the softest rosy white, as, one by one, the blossoms open out.

HENRY BRIGHT
A Year in a Lancashire Garden, 1901

That God once loved a garden
We learn in Holy writ.
And seeing gardens in the spring
I well can credit it.

WINIFRED LETTS
'Stephen's Green'

When rosy May comes in wi' flowers,
To deck her gay, green-spreading bowers,
Then busy, busy are his hours,
The gard'ner wi' his paidle.

ROBERT BURNS

1 May 1903 Cold wind, pelting showers, dull, lowering skies ...

H. RIDER HAGGARD
A Gardener's Year

5 May The garden looks dull just now; but four weeks of no rain always produces that effect on this soil. When the showers do come, everything revives in the most extraordinary way, partly from the earth being so warm and dry.

MRS C.W. EARLE
Pot-Pourri from a Surrey Garden, 1897

It was the morning of the sixth of May,
And May had painted with her soft showers
A garden full of leaves and flowers.
And man's hand had arrayed it with such craft
There never was a garden of such price
But if it were the very Paradise.

CHAUCER
'The Franklin's Tale', *The Canterbury Tales*

The garden record for May ought to be a record of abundance of flowers and rich greenery ... But the May of 1893 will long be remembered as a May in which the garden was burnt up, and everything was thrown out of its proper season.

CANON HENRY ELLACOMBE
In a Gloucestershire Garden, 1895

A gap in the hedge gave a view into the gardens: a border of jasmine, pansies and verbena which ran along the wide path, was interplanted with fragrant wallflowers the faded rose of old Cordoba leather. A long green hose snaking across the gravel sent up every few yards a vertical, prismatic fan, and the multicoloured drops showered over the flowers in a perfumed cloud.

MARCEL PROUST
Du Côté de chez Swann

20 May 1903 On the afternoon I went to Kew Gardens ... The Gardens were looking their very best on this fine spring day, every tree and bush being dressed in vivid green, although here the Chestnuts were not yet blooming. At Kew gardening is really practised as an art.

H. RIDER HAGGARD
A Gardener's Year

21 May I wonder if any effect of bedding is finer than that which my mixed borders have now to show. They are at their very best, for it is the reign of the Paeony and the Iris. Great clumps of each, the one bowed down with the weight of its huge crimson globes, the other springing up erect with its purple-headed shafts, appear at intervals.

HENRY BRIGHT
A Year in a Lancashire Garden, 1879

28 May 1802 The wild columbines are coming into beauty – some of the gowans fading. In the garden we have lilies and many other flowers. The scarlet Beans are up in crowds. It is now between eight and nine o'clock. It has rained sweetly for two hours and a half – the air is very mild.

DOROTHY WORDSWORTH
Journals

7 June 1787 Ice thick as a crown piece. Potatoes much injured and whole rows of kidney-beans killed; nasturtiums killed.

GILBERT WHITE
A Naturalist's Journal

We had not peas or strawberries here till the 8th day of this month. On the same day I heard the first whip-poor-will whistle ... When had you peas, strawberries and whip-poor-will in Virginia? Take notice hereafter whether the whip-poor-will always come with the strawberries and peas ...

THOMAS JEFFERSON
in a letter from New York to his daughter in Virginia, June 1790

Just now the lilac is in bloom,
All before my little room;
And in my flower-beds, I think,
Smile the carnation and the pink;
And down the borders, well I know,
The poppy and the pansy blow ...

ROBERT BROOKE
'The Old Vicarage, Grantchester'

The lilac had almost finished flowering; some of the branches still bore tall mauve chandeliers of flowers in delicate clusters, but in a good many places the balmy spray

which but a week ago was smothering the foliage had withered, shrunk and blackened.

MARCEL PROUST
Du Côté de chez Swann

Soon will the high Midsummer pomps come on,
Soon will the musk carnations break and swell,
Soon will we have gold-dusted snapdragon,
Sweet-William with his homely cottage smell,
And stocks in fragrant blow;
Roses that down the alleys shine afar,
And open, jasmine-muffled lattices,
And groups under the dreaming garden trees,
And the full moon, and the white, Evening-star.

MATTHEW ARNOLD
'Thyrsis'

My sensations are all glossy, spruce, voluptuous, and fine: they wear a candied coat, and are in holiday trim. I see the beds of larkspurs with purple eyes; tall hollyhocks, red and yellow; the broad sunflowers, caked in gold, with bees buzzing round them; wildernesses of pinks, and hot-glowing peonies; poppies run to seed; the sugared lily, and faint mignonette, all ranged in order, and as thick as they can grow.

WILLIAM HAZLITT
looking back on the summers of his childhood, *Why Distant Objects Please*, 1821

As for the roses, you could not help feeling they understood that roses are the only flowers that impress people at garden-parties; the only flowers that everybody is certain of knowing. Hundreds, yes, literally hundreds, had come out in a single night; the green bushes bowed down as though they had been visited by archangels.

KATHERINE MANSFIELD
The Garden-Party

'Tis said, as Cupid danced amongst
the gods, he down the nectar flung,
Which, on the White Rose being shed, made
it for ever after red.

ROBERT HERRICK

The very rose-trees, at which Adam stopped to pluck one, looked as if they grew wild; they were all huddled together in bushy masses, now flaunting with wide open petals, almost all of them of the streaked pink-and-white kind, which doubtless dated from the union of the houses of York and Lancaster.

GEORGE ELIOT
Adam Bede

There was a rose garden all blooming in chorus, and with pillar-roses and arches that were not so much growths as overflowing cornucopias of roses.

H.G. WELLS

Roses red, star-drunken reel
Over trim white garden paths,
White roses in the trellis laths
Glowing bosoms half reveal.

W.J. TURNER

The rose doth deserve the chiefest place amongst all flowers whatsoever; being not only esteemed for its beauty, virtues and fragrant and odoriferous smell but also because it is the honour and ornament of our English sceptre.

GERARD
Herbal, 1597

The rose looks fair, but fairer we it deem
For that sweet odour which doth in it live.

SHAKESPEARE
Sonnets

They that desire to have roses bloom before their neighbours, used to make a trench around the roses a foot deep and into it pour hot water, when the bud of the rose beginneth to be knitted.

PLINY
first to write about the culture of roses

There should be beds of roses, banks of roses, bowers of roses, hedges of roses, edgings of roses, baskets of roses, vistas and alleys of roses.

REVD SAMUEL REYNOLDS HOLE, Dean of Rochester
A Book About Roses, 1869

Only the rose lover can entirely surround and enclose himself in the heart of his flower.

WALTER P. WRIGHT
Roses and Rose Gardens

At this moment [June] the world seems one vast rose-garden.

ALFRED AUSTIN
The Garden That I Love, 1907

Meanwhile, in a cluster of sunbeams, the great White Lily, the old lord of the gardens ... whose patent of nobility dates back to that of the gods themselves ...

MAURICE MAETERLINCK
Hours of Gladness

We once had a lily here that bore *108* flowers on one stalk: it was photographed naturally for all the gardening papers. The bees came from miles and miles, and there were the most disgraceful Bacchanalian scenes ...

EDITH SITWELL

I wish I could in any words paint the hues of these splendid Delphiniums; such shades of melting blue, some light, others dark, some like the summer heaven, and dashed across their pale azure wings with delicious rose.

CELIA THAXTER
An Island Garden, 1894

Here are sweet peas, on tip-toe for a flight,
With wings of gentle flush o'er delicate white,
And taper fingers catching at all things,
To bind them all about with tiny rings.

JOHN KEATS

Such geraniums! It does not become us poor mortals to be vain – but, really, my geraniums!

MARY MITFORD
Our Village

I know nothing so pleasant as to sit there on a summer afternoon, with the western sun flickering through the great elder-tree, and lighting up our gay parterres, where flowers and flowering shrubs are set as thick as grass in a field, a wilderness of blossom, interwoven, intertwined, wreathy, garlandy, profuse beyond all profusion.

MARY MITFORD
Our Village

Midsummer Day 1875 Gathering strawberries. As the day wore the weather became more and more beautiful till at last the evening grew the loveliest I think I ever saw. The rich golden light flooded the lawn.

REVD FRANCIS KILVERT
Diary

Late June, 1899 How beautiful the whole garden looked at the hour when it should have been night, about ten o'clock, in the strange, weirdly daylight! Beyond the high west line of wall and the trees at the upper end, in the cold clear sky lay level flakes of cloud, fired by a sunset glow.

E.V. BOYLE
Sylvana's Letters to an Unknown Friend

5 July 1802 A very sweet morning. William stayed some time in the orchard ... It came on a heavy rain ... The Roses in the garden are fretted and battered and quite spoiled, the honeysuckle, though in its glory, is sadly teazed. The peas are beaten down. The Scarlet Beans want sticking.

DOROTHY WORDSWORTH
Journals

23 July 1765 Hot dry weather still. No rain coming we were forced to put-out more annuals in the dusty border; to shade 'em well, and to give them a vast quantity of water. The garden looks quite destitute of crops ... The ponds in most parishes are quite dried up.

GILBERT WHITE
Garden Kalendar

I had always heard of the brilliant beauty of Scotch gardens, and the moment I saw them I understood why it was. The seasons are so late that all the summer flowers bloom together; May and June of the south merge into July and August in Scotland, and everything is in flower at once. No wonder the gardens look bright; besides, the damp air makes the colours more beautiful and the scent stronger.

MRS C.W. EARLE
Pot-Pourri from a Surrey Garden, 1897

15 August It is, I find, a dangerous thing to leave a garden masterless for even a month. The best of gardens will probably fall short in some respect, and I certainly discover several matters which would have been otherwise had I remained at home.

HENRY BRIGHT
A Year in a Lancashire Garden, 1901

Nature seems to make a hot pause just then – all the loveliest flowers are gone; the sweet time of early growth and vague hopes is past; and yet the time of harvest and in-gathering is not come, and we tremble at the possible storms that may ruin the precious fruit in the moment of its ripeness.

GEORGE ELIOT
Adam Bede

About the edges of the yellow corn,
And o'er the gardens grown somewhat outworn
The bees went hurrying to fill up their store;
The apple boughs bent over more and more;
With peach and apricot the garden wall
Was odorous, and the pear began to fall
From off the high tree with each freshening breeze.

WILLIAM MORRIS
'August'

20 August 1899 Since my last letter there has befallen a disaster, which has worked more ill in the garden than all the long weeks of drought. One night a mighty wind arose which every hour grew in violence till at last the fury of it seemed to know no bounds ... Little wonder that, next morning, when day broke quite calm and still, the lawns were found strewn with green boughs and blossom of the wrecked trees ... And not alone were tall things, such as delphinium, mullein, monkshood, dahlias, etc, prostrate, but also plants of more lowly orders: gallardia, campanulas and even pansies ...

E.V. BOYLE
Sylvana's Letters to an Unknown Friend

My greenhouse is never so pleasant as when we are just upon the point of being turned out of it. The gentleness of the autumnal suns, and the calmness of this latter season, make it a much more agreeable retreat than we ever find it in the summer ... But now I sit with all the windows and the door wide open, and am regaled with the scent of every flower, in a garden as full of flowers as I have known how to make it.

WILLIAM COWPER
in a letter to the Revd John Newton

It was a blustering day and the wind had taken and broken the dahlias. Mrs Honeychurch, who looked cross, was tying them up ...

'Gracious what a mess everything is! Look at my scarlet pompons ...'

E.M. FORSTER
A Room with a View

September About Michaelmas (sooner or later, as the Season directs) the weather faire, and by no means foggie, retire your choice Greens, and rarest Plants (being dry) into your Conservatory.

JOHN EVELYN
Kalendarium Hortense or *The Gard'ner's Almanac*, 1664

Is not October the first of the Months of the Spade – the month when one ought to start trenching and double-trenching, planting bulbs, and doing back-aching things all day to the herbaceous border?

WILFRID BLUNT
A Gardener's Dozen

11 October 1899 Under the influence of all this loveliness, almost I am persuaded to love autumn best, and forget a life-long allegiance to the spring-time of the year. Such infidelity could be brought about by nothing less than a month like this, so wondrously, serenely beautiful. Michaelmas daisies glory in it. Wherever they grow, the garden is a luminous tract of stars, in silvery galaxies of lilac and purple.

E.V. BOYLE
Sylvana's Letters to an Unknown Friend

October Artichokes: tie up the leaves for producing the chard. *Asparagus*: cut down and winter-dress. *Beet*: dig up and lay in sand. *Cabbage*: plant out for the main crop. *Cardoons*: tie up the leaves for blanching. *Carrots*: take up the main crop. *Cauliflower*: prick out under hand-glasses, and into frames. *Cucumbers*: make beds, and sow seed for early crops. *Lettuce*: plant out for the main spring crop. *Parsnips*: take up and preserve in sand. *Potatoes*: take up the main crops. *Tomatoes*: gather the unripe fruit and lay in a forcing-house. *Dig* and *trench* ground during dry weather.

JOHN CLAUDIUS LOUDON
The Suburban Horticulturist, 1842

Who can endure a Cabbage Bed in October?

JANE AUSTEN
Sanditon

Every year, at the season that follows on the hour of the dead, the crowning and majestic hour of Autumn, reverently I go to visit the chrysanthemums ... Their somewhat funereal riches are displayed under the harmonious veil of a November day ...

MAURICE MAETERLINCK
Hours of Gladness

'Tis the last rose of summer
Left blooming alone;
All her lovely companions
Are faded and gone.

THOMAS MOORE
' 'Tis the Last Rose', *Irish Melodies*

The garden was overgrown and deserted. Dead black roses drooped from the unkempt bushes growing over the face of the house, and the broad flagged path was almost hidden by unswept leaves ...

MISS READ
Winter in Thrush Green

In the beginning of this month [November] the appearance of the flower-garden is extremely desolate. The dahlias have generally been seriously injured by the frost, but not quite so much so as to warrant their removal; and a few lingering flowers of other kinds recall melancholy ideas of what has been, but is passed. A mild November is indeed the old age of the floral year; and a sharp frost that kills all the remaining flowers is felt positively as a relief.

JANE LOUDON
Instructions in Gardening for Ladies, 1840

Hurrah! ... it's a frost! The dahlias are all dead.

R.S. SURTEES
Handley Cross

27 November 1782 Fierce frost. Rime hangs all day on the hanger. The hares, press'd by hunger, haunt the gardens and devour the pinks, cabbages, parsley, etc.

GILBERT WHITE
A Naturalist's Journal.

By this time the less devoted gardeners have hung up their tools and retired indoors to continue gardening by the fire.

MARGERY FISH
A Flower for Every Day

The young gardener will have leisure during the long evenings ... to improve himself by reading ... In these days, when the employers of gardeners are readers of gardening books, and often possess a considerable knowledge of vegetable physiology, the young man who does not occupy every moment of his spare time in improving himself, has no chance whatever of getting a good situation as head gardener.

JOHN CLAUDIUS LOUDON
The Suburban Horticulturist, 1842

Foul privies are now, to be clensed and side,
Let night be appointed, such baggage to hide:
Which buried in garden, in trenches alow,
Shall make very many things better to grow.

THOMAS TUSSER
Five Hundred Good Points of Husbandry, 1573

December As no Plant can live without Air, a Gardener must now act with Judgment in helping his Green House Plants; for the Air Abroad is now so sharp, that was it to be lett into the House immediately upon the Plants, it would pinch many of them to Death; and if the Plants were to be shut up for any considerable Time, without recruiting the Air in the House, they would be suffocated.

RICHARD BRADLEY
The Gentleman and Gardener's Kalendar, 1718

There are no flowers that never fade,
yet here are the chrysantheumums,
still blooming in winter.

YUAN HUNG-TAO

14 December 1772 Nasturtiums blow still.

GILBERT WHITE
The Naturalist's Journal

Carry dung into the quarters of your Kitchen-Garden, and spread it upon the ground, and trench up the quarters, laying the earth in ridges, that it may be mellow'd by frost, and be fit for use when the season for cropping them comes on, for if you do not get your ground in readiness at this season, you will have too much business hurrying upon you in the spring.

PHILIP MILLER
The Gardeners Kalendar, 1732

Earthward he boweth the heavy stalks
Of the mouldering flowers;
Heavily hangs the broad sunflower
Over its grave i' the earth so chilly;
Heavily hangs the hollyhock,
Heavily hangs the tiger-lily.

ALFRED, LORD TENNYSON
'Song'

Tennyson ... evidently was not in the habit of making things neat in the garden by cutting down the old flower-stems. If that was his habit, I am much inclined to agree with him; I never think that the prospect of the garden in December is much better by making all the flower-beds too tidy. I feel sure that the dead flower stems ... must be some protection to the plants; and, when the hoar-frosts come, these dead stems, especially where the dead flower-heads remain, put on a wonderful beauty.

CANON HENRY ELLACOMBE
In a Gloucestershire Garden, 1895

For the gardener, winter is a season in its own right, with enough time to seek out the best, often elusive scents, notice the texture of bark, enjoy shadows cast on the lawn by trees and trelliswork.

ROSEMARY VEREY
writing in *The Times*, December 1990

Dilettante gardeners love the spring and summer; real gardeners also love the winter.

ANNE SCOTT-JAMES
Down to Earth

Notwithstanding our disasters born of unseasonable frost and wet, sunless skies, I console myself with the reflection that on the whole we have made good progress. The garden is in better order than it was ... last year.

H. RIDER HAGGARD
A Gardener's Year

A Gard'ner's Work is never at an end; it begins with the Year, and continues to the next.

JOHN EVELYN
Kalendarium Hortense or *The Gard'ner's Almanac*, 1664

It is a greater act of faith to plant a bulb than to plant a tree … to see in these wizened, colourless shapes the subtle curves of the iris reticulata or the tight locks of the hyacinth.

CLARE LEIGHTON
Four Hedges

In the garden snowdrops, crocuses, hyacinths, magnolias, roses, lilies, asters, the dahlia in all its varieties, pear trees and apple trees and cherry trees and mulberry trees, with an enormous quantity of rare and flowering shrubs, of trees evergreen and perennial, grew so thick on each other's roots that there was no plot of earth without its bloom, and no stretch of sward without its shade.

VIRGINIA WOOLF
an amazing garden (every gardener's dream?),
Orlando

Earth laughs in flowers.

RALPH WALDO EMERSON
'Hamatreya'